Pro Stock

By John Hamilton

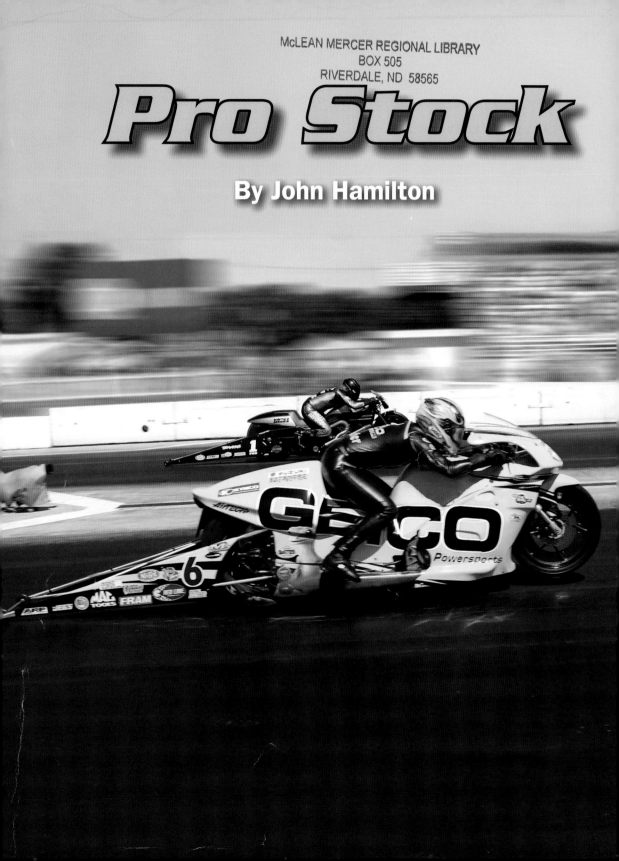

Published by ABDO Publishing Company, PO Box 398166, Minneapolis, MN 55439.
Copyright ©2014 by Abdo Consulting Group, Inc. International copyrights reserved
in all countries. No part of this book may be reproduced in any form without written
permission from the publisher. A&D Xtreme™ is a trademark and logo of
ABDO Publishing Company.

Printed in the United States of America, North Mankato, Minnesota.
112013
012014

 PRINTED ON RECYCLED PAPER

Editor: Sue Hamilton
Graphic Design: Sue Hamilton
Cover Design: John Hamilton
Cover Photo: Corbis
Interior Photos: Alamy-pgs 14-15; AP-pgs 12-13, 25, 26 & 29; Corbis-pgs 1, 2-3,
4-5, 8-9, 16-17, 18-19, 20-21, 27, 28, 30-31 & 32; Getty Images-pgs 6-7 & 22-23,
National Hot Rod Association-pg 24; U.S. Army-pg 10-11.

ABDO Booklinks
Web sites about motorcycles are featured on our Booklinks pages. These links are
routinely monitored and updated to provide the most current information available.
Web site: www.abdopublishing.com

Library of Congress Control Number: 2013946163

Cataloging-in-Publication Data

Hamilton, John, 1959-
 Pro stock / John Hamilton.
   p. cm. -- (Xtreme motorcycles)
Includes index.
ISBN 978-1-62403-221-9
1. Dragsters--Juvenile literature.   2. Motorcycles--Juvenile literature.   I. Title.
629.227/5--dc23

Contents

Drag Racing on Two Wheels

Not all drag racers have four wheels. Pro stock motorcycle racing has exploded in popularity since the 1980s.

Two riders mounted on custom bikes hurtle down a quarter-mile (.4-km) track at more than 195 miles per hour (314 kph). Pro stock motorcycle races are seven seconds of pure adrenaline.

What is a Pro Stock Motorcycle?

Pro stock motorcycles are fast, two-wheeled dragsters. They are sometimes called "factory hot rods" because they look like street motorcycles from manufacturers such as Suzuki, Kawasaki, Harley-Davidson, or Buell. However, these bikes are custom built for racing. To gain extra speed, they use powerful engines, lightweight steel tubing, and aerodynamic bodywork.

Engine and Transmission

The powerful engines used in pro stock motorcycles produce 290 horsepower or more. On-board engine computers capture data about critical functions such as RPM and wheel speed.

For many years, in-line four-cylinder Suzuki engines won many races. Recently, however, Harley-Davidson V-Twin engines have dominated. Rules restricting engine construction are sometimes changed to make competition as fair as possible. Pro stock bikes have transmissions that range from five to seven speeds. Riders shift gears with a handlebar button.

Chassis and Body

Pro stock motorcycles have tubular steel frames. The chassis are adjustable in length, ranging from about 68 to 70 inches (173 to 178 cm). The wheelbase is adjusted depending on track conditions.

Pro stock motorcycle bodies look similar to street bikes, but they are made of lightweight carbon fiber. They are sleek and curved, giving an aerodynamic shape to the bike. Air flows smoothly over and around the motorcycle. When racing, drivers lean forward, further decreasing wind resistance.

Tires

The front tire is used to steer the bike. There is also a shock absorber on the front end, which helps the driver control the bike.

The rear tire on a pro stock motorcycle is bigger than the front tire. Power from the engine is directed to the rear tire, which is 10 inches (25 cm) wide. It is smooth, which gives maximum grip on the track.

XTREME FACT – A pro stock motorcycle tire lasts for about eight drag strip runs.

Wheelie Bars

At the start of a race, a pro stock motorcycle accelerates so quickly that the whole front of the bike lifts up. To keep control of the bike, a "wheelie bar" is attached to the rear. It slams to the ground and prevents the front of the motorcycle from coming up too high.

WAR
White Alligator Racing

USm
401

COMETIC E NP

XTREME FACT—Pro stock riders experience about 3Gs of force when accelerating down a drag strip, about the same force astronauts endured lifting off on the space shuttle!

Safety Gear

In an accident, there are no metal roll bars or seat belts to protect pro stock motorcycle riders.

For safety, riders wear padded full-leather suits that protect the skin when skidding down the asphalt track. Impact-resistant plastic inserts, as well as padded gloves and boots, also give protection. Special helmets with visors protect the head and face.

Burnout

Just before a race begins, riders drive their bikes into the "burnout box."

They spin their rear tire while holding down the brake, keeping the motorcycle in place. Friction causes the tire to heat up and smoke. A hot tire has a better grip on the track during the race.

Staging

At the beginning of the race, the two bikers approach the starting line. This is called staging. Racers watch an electronic device called a Christmas tree. It is a set of multicolored lights between the two racing lanes.

XTREME FACT – If a racer crosses the starting line too early, a red light flashes and the racer is disqualified.

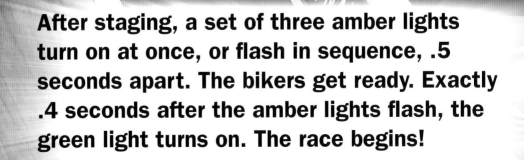

After staging, a set of three amber lights turn on at once, or flash in sequence, .5 seconds apart. The bikers get ready. Exactly .4 seconds after the amber lights flash, the green light turns on. The race begins!

The Race

Pro stock motorcycles accelerate from zero to 100 miles per hour (161 kph) in about two seconds. In just a few seconds, the bikes have traveled to the finish line one quarter mile (.4 km) down the drag strip. Winning times are usually slightly less than seven seconds. Top speeds often reach 195 miles per hour (314 kph) or more.

 XTREME FACT—Pro stock motorcycles must have brakes that are effective enough to safely slow them down from speeds nearing 200 miles per hour (322 kph).

To win, riders need good reaction times at the start, plus good control of their bikes. At such dangerously high speeds, it is difficult to steer. Riders also need to shift gears at just the right time.

The U.S. Nationals

The U.S. Nationals is the biggest and most prestigious drag racing event in the world. It is held each year on Labor Day at Lucas Oil Raceway at Indianapolis, in Indiana. Pro stock motorcycles compete in their own division. Nicknamed the "Big Go,"  the U.S. Nationals is sanctioned by the National Hot Rod Association (NHRA). John Hall of Matt Smith Racing won the event in 2013.

XTREME FACT – Motorcycles first competed at the U.S. Nationals in 1973.

Pro stock motorcycle racer Hector Arana, Sr., competes at the U.S. Nationals race at Lucas Oil Raceway in 2013.

Top Racers

The best time recorded to date of a quarter-mile (.4-km) race is 6.728 seconds. That record was set by Andrew Hines on October 9, 2012, in Mohnton, Pennsylvania. Hines and his brother Matt each hold three NHRA Pro Stock Motorcycle Championship titles.

Andrew Hines

XTREME FACT—Dave Schultz was the most successful pro stock bike racer ever, with six NHRA championship titles. Sadly, he died in 2001, at age 52.

Eddie
Krawiec

The current world speed record is held
by Eddie Krawiec. On March 13, 2011,
in Gainesville, Florida, his motorcycle
reached a speed of 199.26 miles per hour
(320.68 kph). Krawiec won the NHRA Pro
Stock Motorcycle Championship title in
2008, 2011, and 2012.

Several women have been top competitors in pro stock motorcycle racing. Women compete right alongside the men at the drag strip.

Katie Sullivan

Angelle Sampey won the NHRA Pro Stock Motorcycle Championship three times, from 2000 to 2002. She retired in 2010 with 41 career wins. Asked why she loves pro stock bike racing, Sampey said, "I love getting that joy ride. It only lasts seven seconds, but it's the most exciting thing I've ever done."

Angelle Sampey

Glossary

Accelerate
The increasing speed of an object, such as a motorcycle going from a standstill to 100 miles per hour (161 kph) in a short period of time.

Adrenaline
A chemical created in the human body that is released when a person feels strong emotions such as fear or excitement. Adrenaline causes the heart to beat faster and gives a person quick energy.

Aerodynamic
Something that has a shape that reduces the drag, or resistance, of air moving across its surface. Racing bikes with aerodynamic shapes can go faster because they don't have to push as hard to get through the air.

Chassis
The body or frame of a vehicle.

Cylinder
A hollow chamber inside an engine where air and gasoline vapor mix. When ignited by a spark plug, the air/gas mixture explodes, forcing a metal piston inside the cylinder downward. The motion of the piston turns the gears that make the vehicle move.

30

G-Force
A unit of force placed on a body when it is subjected to acceleration. The force is felt as increasing weight. The pull of Earth's gravity equals one G-force.

Horsepower
A unit of measure of power. The term was originally invented to compare the power output by a steam engine with that of an average draft horse.

NHRA
The National Hot Rod Association is the first national drag racing organization. It was formed in 1951 by enthusiast Wally Parks.

RPM
A motor's revolutions per minute.

V-Twin
A common type of motorcycle engine that has two cylinders arranged in a "V" shape.

Index